The

BAR
HOPPER
Handbook

The BAR HOPPER *Handbook*

Scam a Drink, Score a Date, *and* Rule the Night

Written by **BEN APPLEBAUM** *&* **DAN DISORBO**
Illustrations by **DAN DISORBO**

CHRONICLE BOOKS
SAN FRANCISCO

Text copyright © 2014 by Ben Applebaum and Dan DiSorbo.
Illustrations copyright © 2014 by Dan DiSorbo.

Library of Congress Cataloging-in-Publication Data is available.

ISBN: 978-1-4521-1886-4

Manufactured in China

Designed by Liam Flanagan

10 9 8 7 6 5 4 3 2 1

Chronicle Books LLC
680 Second Street
San Francisco, California 94107
www.chroniclebooks.com

*A night out
is a terrible
thing to waste.*

DON'T BE STUPID

Bar Hoppers are fun and social peeps who always party responsibly and in moderation. While bar hopping oftentimes involves drinking alcohol, we do not in any way approve of underage, irresponsible, or excessive alcohol consumption—it is extremely dangerous and no one should do that. Period.

The material contained in this book is presented only for informational and amusement purposes. The publisher and authors do not condone or advocate in any way the use of prohibited substances, underage drinking, or consumption of large quantities of alcohol, and we accept no liability for the consequences of unlawful drinking, overindulgence, or illegal activity of any kind.

So when you bar hop, know your limits, never drink and drive, and never let your friends drink and drive. Use a designated driver system like a smart person, rent a limo like a baller, call a cab like a city slicker, take public transportation like a cheapo, walk like an Egyptian, or sleep it off like a bum; just don't get behind the wheel.

Please hop happily and responsibly!

Contents

INTRODUCTION

There are those who go out to a bar.
   And then there are those who go all out.
There are those who become regulars.
   And then there are those who become legends.
There are those who enjoy a quiet night in.
   And then there are those who don't like any word
   in that last sentence.

Clearly the latter are more fun, more infamous, and more likely to raise roofs with the greatest of ease. So who are they? What makes them tick? And how do you become one?

The answers rest in your hands at this very minute. These consummate party people are Bar Hoppers, and this book is their bible. Well, it's at least their secular-drinking bible. This book may be small in size but it's big in information—the skills, tips, and tricks (literally) that help make any Bar Hopper the master of his domain. And that domain is the bar.

Hoppers are a diverse collective of bar-going, charisma-laden individuals, but they all share similar attributes:

NO 1 ALWAYS UP FOR A GOOD TIME They are ready at the drop of a hat or the text of a phone to go out and get down.

NO 2 NEVER BORED AND NEVER BORING They are able to entertain themselves and others effortlessly. If the scene gets old, they know when to bounce to the next hot spot.

NO 3 ABLE TO PLAY THE SYSTEM To paraphrase the sage rapper Rick Ross, every day I strive to be hustlin' . . . hustlin'. Bar Hoppers don't play by the rules—they bend them in their favor and often in the direction of their wallets.

NO 4 EFFORTLESSLY COOL They know their way around any bar and any crowd. They can be the life of the party without ever breaking a sweat.

But don't let their coolness fool you. Bar Hoppers are not born; they are made. With this volume in your hands, you too can become a pro of the pub, a boss of the bar, and the biggest hole of the watering hole.

Ready? Time to get hopping.

"From there to here,
from here to there,
funny things are everywhere!"

DR. SEUSS

Chapter One

HOPPING

BAR HOPPER BASICS

To truly appreciate the art of bar hopping, first you need to appreciate the science behind it. This chapter provides a crash course of hopping knowledge. It will give you a sense of why you should do it, where you should do it, and who you should do it with. It offers you everything you need to know about building the foundation as an all-pro Hopper. (Everything, except the address for the next hot spot.)

BAR HOPPING DEFINED

At its most basic and awesome level, bar hopping is drinking at multiple bars in one night. Not impressed? While it might not sound epic on paper, the opportunities that multiple locations offer are great and vast. Think of it like an orgasm: One is fun, but multiples are mind-blowing.

BENEFITS OF BAR HOPPING

Now that you know what hopping is, it's time we further explore why it's so important.

NO 1 REFRESHED SURROUNDINGS You can't be bored with so much newness going around. The same old same old will lead to the same old. The Bar Hopper, however, experiences many more new faces, new places, and other new things that rhyme with "aces."

NO 2 PRIME FOR HUSTLING Partying with new people is not just about new scenery. It's about new targets for your scams, schemes, and tricks. You can go pro by trying out all of your old cons. See Chapter 5 (page 69) for more ideas.

NO 3 FREEDOM TO FLIRT The old saw warns you not to shit where you eat. But what about hitting on hotties where you regularly drink? That can be problematic too. Bar Hoppers know this, which is why they take many swings at the plate—more chances to score.

NO 4 BETTER CROWDS TO WORK Bar hopping offers you a chance to make grand entrances and exits. Compared to being stuck in a corner half the night working up the courage to get on the dance floor, hopping is like kicking open the door, grabbing life by the you-know-whats, and rocking out with your inhibitions dismissed. When you're moving on soon, there's no reason to hold back.

NO 5 TASTING TOUR DE FORCE Though your stomach and head may beg to differ, bar hopping is perfect for sampling all the many tastes of these various places. Signature drinks, house specials, famous shots poured from a midget on the bar—all of it rocks.

NO 6 BETTER MEMORIES It's hard to paint the town red from one bar all night—even harder when you're staying in, watching a cop show, and drinking hot cocoa. You need to get out, get together, and get your freak on to make stories that last a lifetime. At least the photo evidence will last a lifetime; the memories might be a bit blurry.

BAR HOPPING vs BAR CRAWLING

Although both have the word *bar* in their name and are often used interchangeably, these two terms could not be any more different from each other. Sure, both involve heading to multiple establishments in one night with multiple friends. But there the similarities end.

Bar crawls are about having as much to drink as possible; *bar hops* are about having as much fun as possible—and drinking is merely a means to this awesome end. The chart below can better compare and contrast these two activities.

BAR CRAWLING

➡ Drink your face off
➡ Planned in advance
➡ Must drink at every bar
➡ Rules on how to keep up
➡ Hang with your group of friends
➡ Stumble home and pass out
➡ Goal: end up horizontal

BAR HOPPING

➡ Laugh your ass off
➡ Planned very little
➡ Probably drink at every bar
➡ Only rule: don't be lame
➡ Make a new group of friends
➡ Bring home those new friends
➡ Goal: stay vertical

FAMOUS BAR CRAWLS

Don't get us wrong: bar crawls aren't bad. In fact, they're a hell of a good time, especially these crawls that top them all.

GATOR STOMPIN'

This annual Gainesville, Florida, tradition dates back more than thirty years and consists of over fifty bars. And you can only imagine the mayhem that ensues when thousands of University of Florida students party simultaneously and competitively.

THE TWELVE BARS OF CHRISTMAS (TBOX)

Since 1996, thousands of Chicagoans have braved the windy chill in Wrigleyville to attend this extreme Xmas celebration. Each year, well over 20,000 revelers attend the celebration— making it one of the biggest crawls of the season.

CHARLOTTE ST. PATRICK'S DAY PUB CRAWL

In 2012, more than 15,000 participants raised pints and a little hell in the Queen City—earning it a world record as the largest pub crawl in the world. Although we think a book with "Guinness" in its title might be biased toward a St. Pat's celebration.

ZOMBIE PUB CRAWL

The first large-scale bar crawl with participants dressed and drinking like the undead was hosted in 2005 in Minneapolis, Minnesota. Today, similar zombie crawls have popped up all over the world—no doubt in search of more brains and more bars.

SEVEN STRATEGIES FOR
SUCCESSFUL BAR HOPPING

Although bar hopping is more spontaneous than bar crawling, one cannot just do it willy-nilly (unless that is the name of a new Bill Clinton–themed bar). Prepare and ensure success with the following strategies.

NO 1 **PICK THE RIGHT PLACE.** It's not enough to pick the right city; you need to pick the right area of the city to ensure optimal hoppability. This critically important decision requires that you look for a place with the following attributes:

PROXIMITY A great area should be close to the location you will be crashing at later. You shouldn't have to travel far to tear it up.

CONCENTRATION When putting one foot in front of the other becomes ever more challenging, the number of bars, clubs, and late-night greasy spoons within walking distance is key.

TOLERANCE You need to be in a community that lets freak flags fly. For example, the town in *Footloose* would be bad since it doesn't allow dancing and it's fictional.

NO 2 ORGANIZE THE RIGHT CREW Bar hopping alone is just wandering around. You need a full-blown entourage to make it epic. But note: a number ain't nothin' but a number, so don't pick quantity over quality. Make sure you have at least two close friends—one responsible associate and one whipping boy or girl to be the butt of the jokes.

SUPER SIDEKICKS

When looking for some hopping buddies, here are sidekicks to seek out:

THE KEY
Gets you into places and gets "stuff"

THE FIXER
Gets you out of trouble

THE LOOKER
Breaks the ice with potential mates

THE DICK
Calls it likes he sees it

THE TIMER
Knows the exact right time to move on

THE ENFORCER
Protects you from fights

THE PUNK
Gets you into trouble

THE DD (DESIGNATED DRIVER)
Sorry, someone has to do it

BAR HOPPING CHECKLIST

Don't leave home, pick up friends, or start bar hopping without it:

CELL PHONES
Batteries charged, times synchronized, ex's numbers removed

STREAMLINED WALLET/PURSE
Cash, one credit card, driver's license, and keys

DRINKING SHOES
Specifically, shoes that are comfortable to walk in after drinking

NO **3** START EARLY TO END LATE A bar hop is not a night out—it's an experience. And one that should, in proper form, start during daylight. We are looking into research about the magical effects on revelers that come from a combo of alcohol and vitamin D. Until then, just know that an early start also positions you better to take advantage of one of mankind's greatest wonders: happy hour.

NO 4   DON'T JUST DRINK, BE THE BAR   A Bar Hopper is not out just to drink (that's his cousin, the bar crawler). A Hopper should be judged not by his ability to get drunk, but by his ability to get jiggy, get freaky, get numbers, get a free beer, and even get thrown out with style. Get it?

NO 5   EAT   An empty stomach can spell the end to the night. And to your decision-making skills. So remember to eat throughout the hopping. A good foundation that's high in carbs and proteins—pizza, anyone?—will ensure that you build a strong structure of awesomeness.

NO 6   PREGAME RESPONSIBLY   Before spending $12 a drink at a bar, consider the pregame. Also known as *preloading, predrinking,* and *prefunking,* this is the strategic use of drinking at home prior to going out. But don't overdo it, or your night will end early and sloppily.

NO 7   COLLECT SOUVENIRS   Some people say you can't take it with you, but they haven't stolen a pint glass from their favorite bar. Souvenirs are not always objects, either. Those insane photos, drunken voicemails, and, most importantly, the friendships forged after a round of tequila shots all should be cherished. And shared.

TOP FIVE CITIES TO BAR HOP

While hopping can happen just about anywhere, here are several cities that rise above the rest:

MANHATTAN

Expensive, yes. Overwhelming, yes. But the public transit and sheer epicness make it a must on everyone's hop-it list.

BROOKLYN

This borough has its own scene—lousy with dive bars, killer food, and plenty of hipsters in their natural environment.

NEW ORLEANS

Sure, you have the French Quarter, but other areas like Frenchmen Street provide less wild and more civilized options.

AUSTIN

More bars than you can shake a rib from a bitching food truck at. More music and weirdness than anyone can experience in a night.

CHICAGO

So many great neighborhoods, from Lincoln Park to Wicker Park to Bucktown. Each with a different flavor for hopping.

THE PREGAME PROTOCOL

Sure, it seems easy and self-explanatory, but there are some rules:

PLAY GAMES

It's the perfect time to break out every drinking game
in the book.*

PLAY IT LOUD

Prepare a playlist that sets the energy and dance moves
for the night.

GO CHEAP

No reason to break out the good stuff. And, remember,
cheap beer, booze, and wine all taste better cold—ice cold.

GO EASY

Pregaming is a great thing, but remember that too
much of a good thing can lead to bad nights and worse
mornings; so drink responsibly.

* *By "the book," we mean* The Book of Beer Awesomeness, *written by, well, us.*

"I get by with a little help
from my friends."

THE BEATLES

Chapter Two

SOCIALIZING

HOW TO MAKE FRIENDS
AND INFLUENCE BARTENDERS

Bar hopping is not a solitary endeavor. Clearly, it's about the friends you choose to carouse with; but it's also about the people you come across. A bar is more than the structure, the drinks, and the stinky bathrooms. A bar is a hodgepodge of humanity—a melting pot of personalities that you can drop into like a bouillon cube. And, while the simile has gotten a bit confusing, it's quite easy to socialize like a pro on your next bar hop using the tips and techniques that follow.

MAKE AN ENTRANCE

A guy walks into a bar . . . So goes the phrase that launched a million jokes. But entering the premises is no laughing matter. In fact, starting your night right is critical. As a wise man—or a commercial—once said, "You never get a second chance to make a first impression." So here are few ways to show up with style.

NO 1 TALK THE TALK A Bar Hopper knows how to roll into a drinking establishment with authority. When entering the bar, make sure you proclaim your arrival for all to hear. But don't let thinking of what to say take up valuable brainpower. Simply choose one of the following Bar Hopper–approved exclamations:

➡ "Let's get this party started."

➡ "Friends, Romans, country-men . . . lend me your beers."

➡ "Let the games begin!"

➡ "It's game time, turds."

➡ "Gather around, children. Daddy is home."

➡ "It's on like Donkey Kong."

➡ "It's on like Alderaan."

➡ "Let's get crackalatin'!"

➡ "The doctor is in."

➡ "Honey, I'm home!"

➡ "Drop your cocks and grab your socks."

WALK THE WALK Making waves when you make an entrance is not hard. All that's needed is some chutzpah and one of the following techniques:

THE RESERVOIR DOGS Just like the criminals in the movie, you and your entourage walk into the bar in self-styled slow motion. It is guaranteed to look much cooler in your head than it will in reality, but who cares about reality, right?

THE BEAT IT This is a throwback to other days, days when men were always dancing. Walk in with your crew to the beat of the music. Leather jackets and a young Michael Jackson are optional.

THE CHAMP Like a prizefighter with his posse, enter the bar as if you were entering the ring. Come to think of it, bar hopping and boxing have a lot in common. They last a bunch of rounds; crowds will cheer on participants; and there's a strong chance participants will be slurring by the end.

THE HUXTABLE The seminal sitcom inspired more than just sweater fashion. The dance moves in the opening sequence provide an endless treasure trove of poses and formations to pull from to make an epic entrance.

THE WILD WEST This, too, is a throwback to the days when men were men, and sanitation was sketchy. Nothing says badass like throwing open the doors and letting your outlaw pose do the screaming.

BREAK THE ICE

A Bar Hopper's great skill is to bring people together, to loosen the mood, and stimulate camaraderie among complete strangers, which is easier said than done—but not with the following tips and tricks.

SAY HI Yeah, it's extremely simple, but that's why it's effective. A simple, "Hey, what's up?" can be all it takes to spark a connection with a new friend (or a friend with benefits).

BRING SOMETHING TO THE TABLE Most people prefer to talk only when there is something to talk about (at least when they're sober). Don't just ask them about the time, the weather, or something else you can find on your iPhone. Talk to them about the important game, the big movie, or even ask them to weigh in on a debate you're having with your friends, and they'll be happy to keep the conversation going.

BAR HOP FACT

The expression *breaking the ice* comes from smashing the ice in cold waters to allow boats to navigate through it—which sounds scary, dangerous, and very much like talking to the wrong crowd.

COMPLIMENT THEM Trite? Yes. Silly? Yes. Effective? You're goddamn right! Nobody can resist the allure of some flattery. Compliment your new connection on something like his choice in sports teams, the fullness of his mutton-chop sideburns, or his preference in beers. Who knows? Maybe they'll be willing to buy you one.

DON'T BE A DOUCHE Starting off a conversation with, "I didn't know this bar let pieces of shit out of the toilet!" likely isn't the best way to win people over, even if you're just joking. Save the disparaging stuff until you at least know their names.

TELL A GOOD STORY, NOT A JOKE Did you hear the one about the blonde who walked into a bar? Of course you did. Only uncles tell actual jokes these days. Instead, retell a story or two.

HOW TO TELL A STORY THAT DOESN'T BORE THE HELL OUT OF EVERYONE BECAUSE IT KEEPS GOING AND GOING . . .

Storytelling is as much a part of bar hopping as beer. Whether it's sharing a trip to Tibet or recounting an ill-fated attempt to do your own taxes, telling a story can win over a crowd.

KNOW THE STORY

They're not paying attention to you just to hear you say, "No, wait; let me start over." Make sure you have your yarn thought out and ready to go before presenting it.

ACT IT OUT

Some people just read a story to an audience—they're called "news anchors." Don't be one. Bring it to life: jump around, flail your arms, shout it out—don't recite it, relive it.

DETAILS, DETAILS, DETAILS

Instead of saying the room smelled bad, describe it as smelling like diapers left out in August on the dashboard of a Buick LeSabre. See, you can almost smell it now.

RESPECT THE STRUCTURE

Go from "meh" to masterpiece by following this classic plot: The hero wants something, but he can't get it, so he does something different and ends up better. It's just that easy.

GIVE A GOOD TOAST

A real Bar Hopper works the bar and everyone in it, making the crowd feel welcome and energized. But that takes more than just Red Bull, though—it takes a great toast to get the night off to a rocking start. Here's how to make a toast everyone will remember, no matter how much they've drunk.

BE AS PREPARED AS POSSIBLE Have a clear idea of what you're going to say before you clang your glass. If you're delivering an impromptu toast, buy some time to compose your spiel by taking a few deep breaths and emphasizing how honored you are.

MAKE EYE CONTACT Look the toastees in the eye at all times. Be sure to engage them with your peepers to let them know this is just for them.

MAKE IT WORTHWHILE If you're making everyone wait a minute before they can drink, be sure to make your toast entertaining.

STRONG FINISH Don't just trail off like some well-wishing zombie. Finish strong and make sure everyone knows your toast is complete by rallying them with a hearty "Cheers!," "Sláinte!," or "Boo-ya!"

COMMON TOASTING TECHNIQUES

While toasts are unique like snowflakes, a savvy Bar Hopper knows how to pull from her bag of tricks and use one of the following classics to get the job done.

THE LATE-IN-THE-NIGHT LOVEFEST
"Serishly, you are like my bestest friends in the whole place."

THE ROAST TOAST
"I'd say Lisa is a great girl, but I don't want to lie to you folks!"

THE TEAR JERKER
(Editor's note: We tried to come up with an example, but only kept making ourselves cry.)

THE HUMBLE BRAG
"A sherpa I met on my last trip to Nepal taught me this toast. . . ."

THE KANYE WEST TOAST
"Imma let you finish your toast about Jim, but Amanda is the most successful person here."

HOW TO BOND WITH A BARTENDER

Your relationship with the bartender is important—very important. They control the booze. Enough said.

NO 1 **COURT THEM EARLY** They work their asses off, and don't need an extra ass to deal with all night. Make eye contact, use their name, make a joke. Yell, whistle, or wave your money? Not so much.

NO 2 **ORDER EASIER** Don't be indecisive. Order clearly and simply. Call the brand if you want it ("Ketel on the rocks"). Know what you want and have your money ready. And always order the same thing for yourself.

NO 3 **PAY SMART** Start a tab. It is easier for them to manage, thus making their life better, thus encouraging them to hook you up.

NO 4 **TIP EARLY** Always tip in cash, and always a bit bigger in the beginning. It sounds antithetical to hustling on the cheap (more on that in Chapter 5), but a $5 tip early can earn you up to $30 in free drinks later.

NO 5 **REAP THE BENEFITS** Many bartenders will hook up a good customer with a free drink. It's called a buyback, and it's a beautiful thing.

"*Persuasion is often
more effectual than force.*"

AESOP

Chapter Three

SCORING

NICELY NUDGING OTHERS
TO GIVE YOU WHAT YOU WANT

Bar Hoppers exude a certain magnetism that tends to elicit gifts from others. Maybe it comes from the charismatic extroversion associated with moving from bar to bar. Maybe it comes from their symbolic heritage of seafaring adventurers who were stopping at the port just long enough to regale the locals with tales of high adventure. Or maybe it's just fun to talk your way into getting stuff. Whether it's cold drinks or a hottie's digits, here are some scoring strategies for Bar Hoppers of all sorts.

HOW TO SCORE A DATE

Scoring someone's phone number is a magical moment, when you've been able to transform them from just a regular person to a potential hookup. Here are several tips for helping you make your move.

NO 1 FOCUS, FOCUS, FOC . . . WHAT? As simple as it sounds, most hitters don't give their full attention to their hittees. Looking over your shoulder for BBDs (Bigger, Better Deals) is a sure way not to seal this one.

NO 2 USE SOME CHEMICAL ENHANCEMENT Not alcohol, but a cheaper chemical: adrenaline. To the human body, arousal is arousal. So if something thrilling is experienced (even if it's just a drinking game), the person is more likely to be attracted to anyone he or she is around at that moment.

NO 3 BREAK OUT THE MAGIC TOUCH Studies report that well-timed touching makes a big impact on how someone perceives you. And before you get excited, this means PG contact. A touch on the forearm or shoulder has been shown to improve feelings such as liking, trust, and a desire to agree to requests.

NO 4 MIRROR, MIRROR Another proven technique is to covertly copy the other person's body language and speech rate. Not obviously, as in a mime class, but subtly, so it triggers the subconscious feelings of similarity, which leads to not-so-subconscious feelings of *bow-chicka-bow-wow*.

NO 5 THE FOLLOW-THROUGH Assuming you are able to get his or her number, do something with it; otherwise you're just some creep collecting phone numbers. A simple text, such as, "It was great to meet you last night," is enough to get the ball rolling.

NO 6 PRESENT A GIFT A foolproof icebreaker is to present a gift. What? You didn't bring one? Well, here's a quick and free trick that will transform a simple paper napkin into a rose. (You can thank us later for this one.)

TOP FIFTEEN PREWRITTEN PICKUP LINES

Sometimes wit, honesty, and being yourself just won't cut it. You need to break out some tried and true pickup lines guaranteed to get a reaction. What kind of reaction? Well, that's to be seen.

- Fat penguin. Sorry, I was looking for something to break the ice.

- I'm suffering from amnesia. Do I come here often?

- My mother told me never to talk to strangers, but I'm going to make an exception in your case.

- I couldn't help but notice you not noticing me.

- If you were any hotter, the sprinklers would be going off right now.

- I never believed in a higher power until I saw you.

- You must be so tired of people hitting on you all night. I know I am.

- Do you believe in love at first sight, or should I walk by again?

- There's something wrong with my cell phone . . . your number's not in it.

- Can I take a picture of you so I can show Santa what I want for Christmas?

- You know, inheriting five billion bucks doesn't mean much when you have a weak heart.

- Do you come here often? Because I think I'm about to.

- What are you doing tonight? Besides me?

- You're so hot, you're melting the elastic in my underwear.

FIVE SCHEMES TO SCORE FREE DRINKS

The kindness of strangers is a precious resource, proof that we are not a cutthroat species that operates at the beck and call of a selfish gene. And this, Hoppers, is exactly why it should be exploited to get free drinks at another's expense. And we do mean expense.

NO 1 BE A FIRST-ROUND HERO There's no better way of stretching your budget than by buying the first round. Choose an inexpensive option like a pitcher of beer and then milk your seemingly generous gesture for the rest of the night as all of your friends follow suit. By the time you approach last call, everyone will be too plastered to recall whether you shelled out for one round or seven.

HOPPER HINT

Get everyone to pose for a picture with your first round—thus making it unforgettable and eminently milkable.

NO 2 USE YOUR UNI Uniforms of all public service, from armed forces to local EMTs, are worth a few drinks. People like to show their appreciation for your hard work through a free drink or two. The acceptable response is, "Thank you, sir/ma'am, I'm not a hero, it's just what I do. And do you mind making that a double?"

HOW TO GET SOMEONE TO BUY YOU DRINKS (FOR WOMEN)

Seems like the most unnecessary section in the history of book sections, but our research shows that many women are not satisfied with the number or quality of drinks coming their way. So here are some pointers:

JUST BE PRESENTABLE

No need to worry about supermodel standards—just put a modicum of effort into your appearance. Guys are simple; anything north of sweatpants will do.

BUT NOT TOO HOT

Most guys aren't looking for a professional—if you know what we mean—so don't go too glam. A little approachable innocence goes a long way.

IF YOU ARE ALONE, DON'T ACT LIKE IT

A single woman in a bar might mean she's either waiting for someone or waiting to get picked up. This causes pause—and that can reduce the chance of a free drink.

IF YOU'RE IN A GROUP, BREAK AWAY

A large pack of females can be intimidating to approach—not to mention expensive to buy drinks for. So if you are rolling with your full posse, break off into a *possette* of two or four friends to be more free-drink worthy.

HOPPER HINT

Make sure you actually see your "free" drink being poured by the bartender. Some scumbags put other things in drinks and you need to watch out. Sorry for the buzzkill, but it happens.

NO 3 **BE HOT** Sure, the meek get the Earth, but the good-looking will get the Long Island Iced Teas. It's not fair, but it's fact. Studies show that good-looking people are perceived as more likable and honest. So start looking hotter.

NO 4 **JUST ASK** Just put it out there. Rather than beat around the bush—or the Busch Light—put your request out there in an entertaining way and see who steps up to the pint. Below are fifteen lines you might use.

➡ Excuse me, I'm collecting drinks for the poor and was wondering if you'd like to contribute to our fund?

➡ This isn't a beer belly, it's the fuel tank for my love machine, and I'm down a quart. Care to help me fill up?

➡ I bet you a beer you're gonna turn me down.

➡ Why, yes, you can buy me a drink. Thank you for asking.

➡ You know, you'd be a lot more attractive if you bought me a beer.

➡ This is going to sound crazy, but I've never tried alcohol before. What's it like?

- You're going to have to buy me a drink because I dropped mine the moment I saw you.

- Remember the IOU that I gave you? It's time to make it U owe Me . . . a beer.

- I'm looking for someone to anchor my drinking team. Why don't you buy me a beer, and we'll talk about your prospects.

- Remember that kid you used to sponsor in Africa? He said he's doing fine now and wants you to sponsor me instead.

- A friend in need is a friend indeed, and right now I seriously need another beer.

- Silence is golden, and my silence can be bought for a beer.

- Would you like to make a donation toward my ongoing war on sobriety?

- I think I'm about to die of thirst. You wouldn't want that on your conscience, would you?

- Everybody has to believe in something. I believe I'll let you buy me a drink.

NO **5** CHARM THE PINTS OFF THEM Sometimes the best way to get a free drink from a stranger is to be so damn likable and fun, they just can't help but buy you a cold one. The trick is to establish an instant rapport and step out of the way as the free drink express pulls into the station.

HOW TO SOCIAL-ENGINEER YOUR WAY TO A FREE BEER

By Christopher Hadnagy, Social Engineer

First, let me define what I mean by this. I define **social engineering** as any action that influences a person to take an action that may or may not be in their best interest.

In essence, we are talking about getting someone to have the idea that it is in their best interest to part with beer on our behalf. But the question still arises why anyone would want to part with such sweet nectar for someone they may not even know?

The first rule to remember is, people like people who like them (I know, I sound like a drunken Yoda). If you can make someone feel liked, then they will like you; and if people like you, they will want to do things for you.

Once, I walked into a bar on a business trip and sat down next to a small group of people who weren't really chatting, just light talk and drinking. The bartender came up, and I ordered water.

After a few minutes, I turned slightly toward the group next to me and said, "Excuse me, I have to head out soon, but I have never been here before. Can you help me for a second?" Mentioning that I needed to leave shortly did a couple things: First, it made the issue at hand (my drink choice) seem pressing. And second, it made the group breathe easy, knowing that if I turned out to be a weirdo, I wasn't going to try to hang around with them all night.

I knew I had some interest from them when two people in the group turned totally toward me; so I turned slightly more toward them. "Sure, what's up?" one perky girl asked.

"Well, I travel a lot for business and when I go to new places I like to try new beers. What local beer do you think is the best here?"

The one girl tells me she has lived here her whole life and then proceeds to tell me about two or three beers she loves. She is now the "expert," so when she mentions a beer, I interject a question to keep her talking, such as, "Is that a wheat beer?"

After listening to her for about seven minutes I say, "Which one of those is your favorite?" She talks for three more minutes without taking a breath and then says, "Oh my God, here I am talking and you don't have your beer. . . ." She points to the bartender and says, "Get him a bourbon ale on me." Once I had given her the gift of listening to her, she felt she needed to reciprocate with a far more glorious gift—the gift of free booze.

Christopher authored Social Engineering: The Art of Human Hacking *and runs a firm that protects companies from malicious hackers at www.Social-Engineer.com*

FOUR SIMPLE SCAMS FOR THE BAR HOPPER

A Yiddish proverb states that a half-truth is a whole lie. But it doesn't mention that a whole lie can turn into a full beer. While a *scheme* is a bit underhanded in getting compliance, a *scam* is overhanded in its pursuit of the goal: free stuff that makes your head spin around.

NO 1 THE BOGUS BIRTHDAY SCAM Let's take the sage advice of one 50 Cent to party like it's your birthday even though we don't give a darn that it's not really your birthday. Everyone likes to celebrate with a birthday boy or girl, and it's a great way to get a drink for free. Occasionally you might also get a bonus dessert and a begrudging song from the waitstaff. To pull this off, you need to go over the top in wardrobe and behavior: consider a tacky "Happy Birthday" shirt and "Look Who's Forty" mug. If you look ridiculous enough, they won't question you.

HOPPER HINT

Go the extra step and rent a limo: safety and a better cover.

___

NO 2 **THE FAKE BACHELOR/BACHELORETTE SCAM** This is like the birthday scam, but the celebration is wilder, so expect more shots, more toasts, more affection, and possibly more cold sores. The beauty is that, unlike the risk of someone calling BS on your birthday, there is no documentation for engagement. All it takes is commitment, some embarrassing clothes, and an ironclad story. And for women: a cheap fake engagement ring.

NO 3 **THE ARRANGED ACCIDENT** Polish off three-quarters of your water with lime and "accidentally" bump into another patron. The contact must be convincing, and it should result in you immediately losing the contents of your now "vodka and soda" on the floor below. If your victim is a decent human being, he'll offer to buy you another round and may even invite you to join his group. Don't try this too close to the bar, because the tender will call your bluff. And don't try this too late at night with a meathead, because the dude will call you out and beat your face in. Other than those ground rules, you are home free.

NO 4 — THE BEERAMID SCHEME

Hoppers can learn a lot by spreading their wings and learning from some of the best scammers in the game—businessmen! And one of the best tools is the Ponzi, a.k.a. pyramid—ahem, *beeramid*—scheme.

THE PITCH Start by calling up a buddy to meet you at your favorite bar. Insist that if he pays for the first round, he won't have to pay for another drink the rest of the night.

THE RECRUIT Have another friend meet you (or scout out a lone wolf) at the next bar. Tell this new drinking buddy you're doing an exclusive bar hop where the drinks are *almost* free and the initiation for new members is to buy the first round.

THE PYRAMID After that, the lowest member will do all the recruiting at each new bar you go to, because they now want to make sure they're getting their free drinks. Like all Ponzi schemes, this beeramid will eventually collapse; but, since you're at the top, you will never have to spend a hard-earned cent.

The word *bum* connotes a backside. But the art of bumming takes other body parts to pull off—brains and brass balls. It requires more finesse than other techniques, so here are some helpful tips for bumming your ass off.

DRINK When a person asks you to watch their drink, watch it go all the way into your mouth. When they come back, remind them not to trust you.

FOOD Pretend you've never tried a food before. Feign amazement and disbelief. ("*Pee-za*? Funny name and it's weird-looking, it can't possibly taste good.") People will offer you a taste just to witness your reaction.

SMOKE Pretend to have been trying to quit and act "pained" when you ask for a smoke. They will feel both pity and satisfaction when you are back on the dark side.

TOKE Elise McDonough of *High Times* offers this advice: "Bumming toke requires a level of finesse. If you can trade something, like food or a few beers, that really helps."

TRANSPORTATION Only have enough money for food or a cab? Do both. Walk to a pizza shop and call in a delivery to your house. Get a ride with the delivery guy.

"The money's the same, whether you earn it or scam it."

BOBBY "THE BRAIN" HEENAN

Chapter Four

WINNING

TRICKS AND BETS TO SCORE FREEBIES

Seasoned Bar Hoppers do not see a pub; they see a jackpot. Sure, you could always spend your own money during the night out, but that's like going to Vegas and playing the change machine—no risk, but no fun. This chapter will outline some of the easiest, quickest, and sleaziest ways to snag some freebies using only good old-fashioned trickery, word play and, of course, charisma.

RULES OF THE GAME

For our purposes, sucker bets are meant to be fun and lighthearted. Nothing good ever happens when you scam for serious money—you want to keep all your fingers, right? Here are some quick tips to keep yourself out of a potential bar fight.

➡ You perform sucker bets at your own risk.

➡ Performing these scams on your friends and family is fun. Performing them on complete strangers is risky.

➡ Make sure you know who you're playing against. Pulling one of these tricks off on, say, a "connected" customer could end in a date with a horse's head.

➡ Don't hustle too much in one place. You don't want a bunch of your victims teaming up to give you an all-star ass whooping.

➡ When in doubt, take off and just keep hopping.

PROPOSITION BETS AND BAR TRICKS

Proposition bets, a.k.a. "prop bets," are challenges that reap a reward if successfully performed. Luckily for you, your victims will fail almost all of these (unless they read this book first, of course). So get ready and grab your thirst for victory, because you're about to scam some chumps.

Rollin' Dolla Bills, Y'all

WHAT YOU'LL NEED

➡ Empty beer bottle

➡ Dollar bill

THE SETUP Lay the bill down flat and stand the bottle upside down, on its top, in the center of the bill.

THE BET You can remove the bill from under the bottle without knocking over the bottle and without touching the bottle.

THE TRICK In this classic bar bet, all you need to do is roll the bill from one end. Once the rolled bill reaches the bottle, continue to roll slowly and the bill will push the bottle as it slides from underneath it—just be careful not to touch the bottle with your hands.

BONUS BOOTY

Sometimes a free drink might not be what you're looking for. In those rare cases, here is a list of other prizes worthy of a Hopper's pursuit:

- CASH MONEY
- BRAGGING RIGHTS
- DIGITS OF A POTENTIAL HOOKUP
- A RIDE HOME
- A SANDWICH
- A KISS
- THE HELL OF IT

Pimp Slap

WHAT YOU'LL NEED
- Empty beer bottle
- Dollar bill
- Quarters

THE SETUP Balance the dollar bill on top of the bottle, place the quarters (three or four will do) on top of the dollar so they are centered over the bottle's opening.

THE BET You can remove the dollar bill without knocking the coins off the bottle, using only one finger.

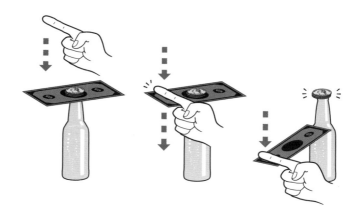

THE TRICK Lick your pointer finger and quickly slap that moistened finger down on one end of the dollar bill. The dollar bill will be pulled free, and the coins will remain on top of the bottle. This one takes some extra practice, so be sure you get the technique down before you attempt to hustle anyone—otherwise, you'll look like some fool with a spit-covered finger.

HOPPER HINT

If you perform a hustle and your mark gets pissed, a good way to talk your way out of a bloody nose is to tell him to think of his loss as tuition for the education you just gave him. So you deserve a thank-you instead of a haymaker.

WHAT YOU'LL NEED

➡ Three full pints of beer

➡ Three full shots of booze

THE SETUP Order up three pints of your favorite beer and three of your victim's favorite shots, and line them up in a row.

THE BET You can drink your three pints of beer faster than your victim can drink his three shots. To be fair, neither of you may touch the other's glass, and your victim can't drink his first shot until you finish your first pint. Whoever loses has to pay for the other's drinks.

THE TRICK Drink the first pint of beer and quickly place the empty pint upside down over one of the shot glasses. Since your victim can't touch your glass, they can't drink the shot. Now you can enjoy your other two beers in a leisurely fashion while your frustrated opponent watches (and wallows) in defeat.

You and a buddy are bar hopping one cold night, and when you get to your last spot, you bet your buddy a round that he's too drunk to take his jacket off by himself. Obviously, he's going to take that bet and, as soon as he starts taking off his jacket, you start taking yours off at the same time. Technically he's *not* taking it off by himself. Sucker! It's all in the wording.

Snifter Shifter

WHAT YOU'LL NEED

➡ A snifter or red wine glass (needs to be a bulb-shaped glass)

➡ An olive or a cherry or even a bottle cap

➡ Another empty glass of any kind (used as a decoy)

THE SETUP Place the olive on the table with a glass on either side.

THE BET You can get the olive off the table and into one of the glasses without touching it with your hands or any body parts. The olive can touch only one glass at a time, and you can't scoop it with the glasses or roll it off the table into a glass.

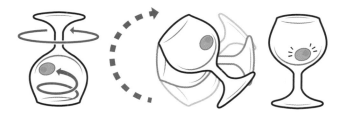

THE TRICK Place the snifter/wineglass upside down over the olive and slowly begin to rotate/spin the glass, keeping the rim on the table. The olive will begin to roll around and rise upward to the widest part of the glass (thank you, centrifugal force!). With the olive rolling around, quickly flip the glass over and the olive will remain inside the glass.

QUICKIE: **ALL FOLD UP**

Find a big piece of paper. Your old 'N Sync poster, a paper placemat, or a piece of newspaper will do fine—the bigger and thinner, the better. Bet your mark that he can't fold the paper in half more than nine times. Watch and laugh as your opponent fails to fold the paper in half more than nine times because it's physically impossible to do so—no matter how big or thin the sheet is. Next, bet him that he can't fly—he may take that bet, too.

Turning Water into Whiskey

WHAT YOU'LL NEED

→ A shot glass full of whiskey

→ An identical shot glass full of water
  Make sure both shot glasses are exactly the same size
  and shape.

THE SETUP Place the two shots side by side.

THE BET As if you were the Jesus of Kentucky, you can turn
the whiskey shot into water, and the water shot into whiskey, without drinking either or using any other glasses.

THE TRICK Place a smooth laminated card, such as your
driver's license or a playing card, over the mouth of the water
shot. (A credit card with raised numbers won't work.) Very
carefully, turn the shot upside down, using the card to keep

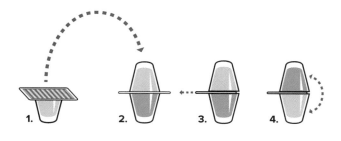

anything from spilling. Now place the upside-down shot and card over the whiskey shot—making sure to align them perfectly. Pull the card slowly out to the side, so there's a tiny crack between the glasses. The whiskey will begin to funnel up through the crack and into the water, which in turn will fall into the bottom glass. Behold the might of Science!

QUICKIE: **MATCH DROP**

Pull a single match out of a matchbook. Wager your opponent that you can drop the match on its thinnest side (as opposed to its flat side) and get it to stand. Give them a few shots at doing the trick themselves, so that they realize it's impossible. Once they give up, bend the match into an "L" shape. Now the match will almost certainly land on its thinnest side, and you will almost certainly collect a free drink.

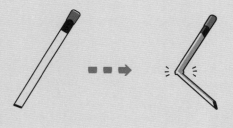

QUICKIE: **BOTTOMS UP**

Present an unopened bottle of wine or champagne to the fool silly enough to bet against you. Bet that you can drink from the sealed bottle without ever opening it. Wine, champagne, and many other liquor bottles have a deep concave at the bottom of the bottle. Tilt the bottle upside down, pour your real drink into the concave, and sip away. Enjoy watching your mark try (and fail) to call you out on the bet.

Poppin' Bottles

WHAT YOU'LL NEED

➡ An unopened beer bottle (not a twist-off)

➡ A paper napkin

THE SETUP Show off your napkin and beer bottle and nothing more.

THE BET You can open the beer bottle with just a napkin.

THE TRICK Fold the napkin in half diagonally, then roll it up *very* tightly, starting at the wide end. Fold it once more after it's rolled and make sure the folded joint is tight and flat. Stick that part under the teeth of the bottle cap and use your index finger (the one wrapped around the bottle neck) as a leverage point. The napkin becomes a lever, the beer becomes open, and you become one freebie richer.

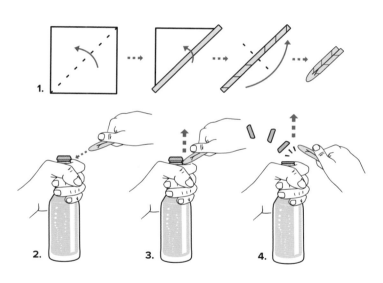

1.

2.

3.

4.

Re-Rack

WHAT YOU'LL NEED

➡ 10 plastic cups ready for some beer pong

THE SETUP Rack the cups backward (4 in the front, then 3 behind them, then 2, then 1 in the back) on the beer pong table.

THE BET Bet your confused opponents that they can't make the triangle face the right direction in three moves or fewer.

THE TRICK After watching them curse and scratch their heads, simply move the cups at the tips of the rack. See the illustration to see how simple it is.

Spit or Swallow?

➡ Two shots of your favorite hooch

THE SETUP Put one shot in front of you and one in front of your opponent, and challenge him to a game of "Monkey See, Monkey Do."

THE BET Wager that your victim can't mimic every move you do.

THE TRICK Perform some random moves, such as scratching your head, blinking your eyes, sticking out your tongue, etc., while your victim mimics each one. Take the shot as a move, but covertly don't swallow. Add a few more gestures, then spit the shot back into the glass. Your victim won't be able to mimic because . . . he swallowed. Winner!

"*Things may come to those who wait, but only the things left by those who hustle.*"

ABRAHAM LINCOLN

Chapter Five

HUSTLING

HOW TO WIN A FEW MORE

Not satisfied with mere parlor tricks, some Bar Hoppers prefer games with higher stakes. Being able to go all *Color of Money* on someone at a bar is not something you can just learn in a book (or, in this case, an '80s Tom Cruise movie). But what a book can do is provide some insight and inspiration into the world's third-oldest profession: hustlin'. And that's just what this chapter will do.

ART OF THE SANDBAG HUSTLE

Sandbagging is an art. Like any art form, it takes natural talent. But it also takes practice. Thankfully the basic principles are simple. Just follow the structure below to become a modern-day Leonardo da Vinci . . . or at least a modern-day Leonardo who doesn't feel like paying for a beer. Here are the basic principles:

PRACTICE! Hustling is 50 percent skill and 50 percent acting like you have *no* skill—and you need to be damn good at both! For instance, if you're hustling a basketball game, make sure you play like Shaq and act like, well, anybody *but* Shaq (anyone who has seen *Steel* or *Blue Chips* knows what we're talking about).

PICK A TARGET You can't hustle if you can't win; so make sure you stake out all possible competition for an easy target. The ideal opponent is someone who can keep up with you, but can't surpass you. Take significant time to watch the other players so you can single out an (un)worthy competitor.

FEIGN DEFEAT Once you have an opponent, engage him in a friendly game or two, and let him win by a small but noticeable margin. This will let his ego inflate, making him more comfortable to accept a friendly wager.

PACE YOUR BETTING AND YOUR WINNING Keep the first bet small, simple, and affordable, and keep the spread on your wins marginal. This will prevent your opponent from losing nerve after the first defeat and, if you're lucky, motivate him into . . .

DOUBLE OR NOTHING! After you've inflated your opponent's ego and then challenged it, he's going to feel the need to prove himself to you and his peers. This is the ideal situation to challenge him double or nothing, thus increasing your winnings. Goad him into betting the farm, and go in for the kill!

COMMON SANDBAG HUSTLES

When hopping, you'll notice that two games reign supreme: pool and beer pong. These bar sports are prime for hustling, so be prepared and be somewhat good at them if you plan to get your hustle on.

POOL Pool is a game of balls and shafts. Wait—that came out all wrong! Let's just move on. The unpredictability of the balls as well as the challenge of mastering physics makes pool a game that's easy to learn, difficult to master, and incredibly fun to hustle.

HOW TO HUSTLE In order to mislead your opponent, start off by missing the easy shots early and often while occasionally making a trickier shot "by accident," swearing it's a fluke. This will help to further boost your opponent's confidence.

HOW TO WIN A surefire way to hustle a victory in pool is by "potting" your balls—in other words, hitting it just right so that it stops just before the pocket. On the surface, this will make you look like a rookie who doesn't know how to follow through on her shot; however, on a more masterful level, this technique actually allows you to block the pocket from your opponent while setting the ball up for an easy sink later in the game.

EXPRESS POOL HUSTLES

Sure, you can practice for years to be able to hustle someone at pool. Or just try these tricks that take the skill out of the hustle and replace it with some good, old-fashioned trickery!

INSTANT SINK

Start by betting your opponent that you can sink a ball on the break. When he confidently takes the bet, have him rack the balls as he would in any other game. When you go for the break, take a nice, easy shot at the cue ball and knock it into the pocket of your choice. Hey, you never specified *which* ball you would knock in on the break.

BALLS DEEP

Lay the cue stick across the width of the pool table. Then bet that you can roll the cue ball underneath the cue stick without holding the stick and without the ball touching the stick. Have the poor fool you're hustling try to roll the cue ball underneath the stick, which they won't be able to do because the space between the stick and the tabletop is too small. Show them how it's done by picking up the cue ball and rolling it on the floor under the table so it technically rolls under the stick without ever touching it.

BEER PONG The sport of champions, beer pong involves two opponents each sinking their (Ping-Pong) balls into their opponent's cups. For each cup made, the opponent drinks the cup's contents, which is usually beer. First to sink their balls into all of the opponent's cups wins.

THE CHALLENGE A major strategy of beer pong is to fight through the decreased motor skills that come with the constant beer consumption, meaning most players try to win by building up a strong alcohol tolerance.

HOW TO HUSTLE Feign drunkenness so that the opponents can relax and let their drunkenness set in. Once you see them swaying and slurring, go for the kill and start sinking balls like they are the *Titanic*.

OTHER TERMS FOR A HUSTLER

BILKER	GRIFTER	RAPSCALLION
CHARLATAN	HOSER	SCAMMER
CHISELER	LOUSE	SHARK
CONNIVER	MALINGERER	SHYSTER
DODGER	PETTIFOGGER	SWINDLER
FLEECER	QUACKSALVER	TRICKSTER
FLIMFLAMMER		WEASEL

THE BEEER PONG METHOD

The mechanics of your beer pong shot is key to being a great shooter rather than an amateur chucker. To help you master the complexity of the beer pong shot, we've created a patented breakthrough acronym to help you out: BEEER

 B **BALANCE** Make sure you are perfectly balanced before you attempt a shot.

 E **EYES** Focus and aim on the back rim of one specific cup while you shoot.

 E **ELBOW** Keep your elbow in toward your body while shooting to reduce shot variability (and keep your elbow behind the table to avoid any rule disputes).

 E **EXTEND** Straighten your arm as you release the ball and follow through.

 R **REMEMBER** Remember the preceding four points for every shot.

"*Why not show off if you've got something to show?*"

JANUARY JONES

Chapter Six

SHOWING OFF

HOW TO BE
THE LIFE OF THE PARTY

A Bar Hopper doesn't want to just go into an establishment. He wants to own it (metaphorically speaking, of course). It's all about the transformation from commoner to pub royalty—and the transformation of an everyday evening into a once-in-a-lifetime experience. Going from just a patron to the patron saint of awesome is no small feat, but the Bar Hopper with the right combination of motivation, talent, strong drinks, and the contents of this chapter might just make it happen tonight.

BECOME A KARAOKE GOD

The word *karaoke* is a mash-up of the words for "empty" and "orchestra" in Japanese. But there is nothing empty, or as formal as an orchestra, about rocking out when you're bar hopping. Due to the time commitment and liquid courage required, the karaoke sessions often come at the end of the bar hop. But don't expect to rock out without some preparation.

NO 1 DON'T HANG BACK Legendary bar hopping is about going all-out when you go out. And the makeshift karaoke stage is no different. If you half-ass it, you'll make a full ass of yourself. So get up and sing your ass off.

NO 2 PICK FOR POPULARITY Choose a song everyone will know. Sarah Lewitinn, author of *The Pocket DJ* and a karaoke expert, sums it up: "If you choose a song that they know, they'll get to feel like they're having their turn and take the pressure off you."

NO 3 LEAVE THEM WANTING MORE Keep it short and keep the crowd on your side. According to Sarah, "The biggest mistake that people make is choosing a song that's over five minutes . . . unless the track is Bonnie Tyler's masterpiece 'Total Eclipse of the Heart.'"

NO 4 KNOW YOUR FLOW Make sure you know the lyrics like the back of your repeatedly bar-stamped hand. "There's nothing more awkward than standing around and stumbling on the words," notes Sarah.

NO 5 ROCK OUT WITH IT ALL OUT Above all else, karaoke should be executed with visceral intensity. This is not an audition, and a British judge will not critique your pitch. No, this is a time to release your inner rock god: thrust your pelvis, gesticulate with passion, and, by all means, sweat with effort.

AN EXPERT'S
KARAOKE PLAYLIST

By Sarah Lewitinn, author of The Pocket DJ

THE KILLERS, "MR. BRIGHTSIDE"
I know all the words and I have an alto voice (or something),
so my vocals work better with men's voices.

DAVID BOWIE, "ZIGGY STARDUST"
This song is about a crazy rock star, so it's a great song for
putting on a fun performance. I suggest that if you choose this
song you should listen to the Bauhaus version.

SPICE GIRLS, "WANNABE"
Every girl knows all the words. Plus, you can sing it with
a group of your friends instead of having the spotlight all to
yourself (if you want to share).

SALT-N-PEPA, "SHOOP"
Try singing this song in any setting without everyone
(or at least the girls) jumping in to sing along. Just try it.
It won't happen. This is a real crowd pleaser.

NEIL DIAMOND, "SWEET CAROLINE"
Under four minutes long and with the always-crowd-pleasing
refrain, "Bah bah bah."

VANILLA ICE, "ICE ICE BABY"

You know all the lyrics to this awesome song, and that's nothing to be ashamed about.

OASIS, "WONDERWALL"

Once I was in a bar when this song came on, and everyone started singing along, and there wasn't even any karaoke going on. That's how you know it's a great karaoke song.

THIRD EYE BLIND, "SEMI-CHARMED LIFE"

I select this song whenever I want to blow everyone's mind, because anyone who was a teenager in the '90s secretly loves it.

MADONNA, "LIKE A PRAYER"

This breaks my "no song over five minutes" rule; but, holy jeebus, this song is awesome. I pick it when I've had too much to drink and have no regard for anyone around me.

THE ISLEY BROTHERS (OR THE BEATLES), "TWIST AND SHOUT"

The song is 2:33 minutes of pure fun and awesomeness. When performing it, you're essentially ordering people to have fun. And they do.

Read more of Sarah's expert music commentary at ultragrrrl.com

TEARING UP THE DANCE FLOOR

A Bar Hopper must be comfortable with all things in the bar. In addition to the drinks and the games, they need the moves—never huddling in the corner but going all in on the dance floor. Joining a gyrating crowd is one thing. But the real stardom comes from ruling the dance floor with an iron hip thrust and earning praise from fellow revelers. So, here are a few tips for putting more *oogie oogie* into your boogie.

DANCING FOR YOURSELF Never, ever care about what anyone else thinks. Trying too hard to fit in will only make you stand out more. You have an inner funky child just waiting to get out.

OOZE CONFIDENCE The crowd is like a wild beast: it's sweaty, hairy, and can smell fear. So make sure every pore is oozing self-assuredness. To this end, don't look down at your feet, don't hesitate when it's your turn, and don't slip when you climb up on the bar to get down.

LEAVE IT ON THE FLOOR There are no doggy bags for the Bar Hop. So go all out, don't pull punches, only pull the occasional hamstring.

TYPES OF
DANCING FORMATIONS

*Before you can rule the dance floor,
you need to be able to spot the different dance formations.*

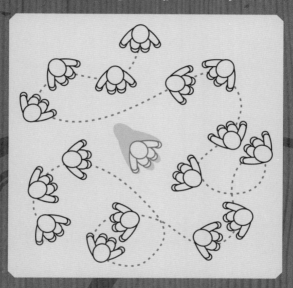

OPEN SWIM

Get your back up off the wall and dance.
This free-form free-for-all is fun but difficult to rule,
since there is no clear place in the spotlight.

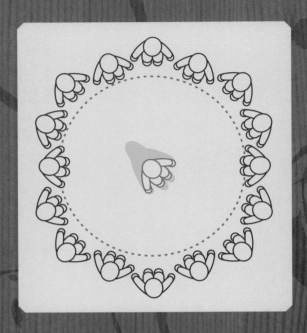

THE CYPHER

A circle area is cleared on the dance floor and dancers take turns
jumping into the middle, tearing it up, then exiting to make room
for the next dancer. It's the perfect chance to take center stage.

THE SOUL TRAIN

The crowd forms two lines, and couples dance down
this "human hallway." It provides the perfect showcase
for busting moves and bumping hips.

TOP SHOWCASE DANCE MOVES
(FOR THE NONDANCER)

If you already have moves like Jagger, then you don't need
to preplan the show-stopping dance you'll break out when
the crowd is watching. But, for the rest of us, here are four
handy moves that require more balls than talent.

THE WORM Sure it requires strength and flexibility, but it
thankfully doesn't require rhythm—a much rarer resource.
Start in push-up position and kick your legs back off the
ground, lifting up your hips and undulating your body
across the dirty floor.

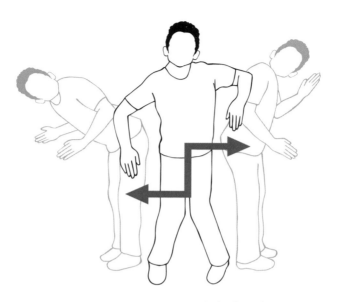

THE MALFUNCTIONING ROBOT To do the robot correctly takes practice and muscle control; but to do it poorly, it just takes some guts and the ability to move with sharp, angular motions. Simply move like C-3PO to the beat. To end it with some shine, convulse like you're about to self-destruct.

THE THRILLER While the whole choreography from "Thriller" would be time-consuming to learn, the creepy fingers and sideways walk are easy and always a hit. Mash it up with some Crunk craziness and you will be that much closer to the bar-dancing Hall of Fame.

THE ROW ROW While you're getting messy on the floor, you can shut down any dance-off by doing this move, which combines a scooting-on-your-butt action with a rowing arm motion that looks so stupid you have to applaud it.

AVOID THESE MOVES

Consider yourself warned. Bar Hoppers pledge to keep these moves from ever being busted again.

THE SPRINKLER

THE SHOPPING CART

TWERKING
(ESPECIALLY IF
YOU'RE MALE)

THE SATURDAY
NIGHT FEVER

THE CABBAGE PATCH

ANYTHING THAT PRO-
DUCES THE "WHITE-
GUY OVERBITE"

SURVIVE A SPICY CHALLENGE

Sometimes the greatest showstopper is quiet, focused, and possibly life-threatening. Many bars promote their infamous eating challenges, usually involving particularly spicy hot wings. If one of the bars on your hop has one, it is your moral imperative as a Bar Hopper to sack up, step up, and shine like a star.

NO 1 DON'T EAT ON AN EMPTY STOMACH Lay the foundation for the fire with neutral and absorbent vittles like banana and white bread.

NO 2 PROTECT YA LIPS A thick coating of lip balm (or Vaseline) will keep this sensitive tissue safe. The other sensitive tissue, you're on your own.

NO 3 SHAKE IT UP The active ingredient in peppers is capsicum, which is not water-soluble, so water won't work. Try something with fat and sugar, like a cold milkshake to cool off.

NO 4 TAKE YOUR MEDS Have at the ready some antacids and heartburn pills to make the flame less eternal.

DRINK AN INFAMOUS DRINK

Sometimes getting everyone's attention and adulation is a feat of daring—in a glass. These drinks are seen as mini-Everest summits, and all eyes are on whoever will be brave enough to step up.

EAT THE TEQUILA WORM This infamous act is the universal symbol for "Badass on Board." Never mind that the worm is actually a butterfly larva. And the liquid is not tequila, but its less regulated cousin, mescal. The only fact that you need to worry about is making sure everyone sees you with the worm in your mouth and party in your heart.

DRINK THE MAT It goes by many names: Suicide Shot, Alligator Fart, Matt Dillon, and even the Jersey Turnpike. Regardless of the name, the process is the same: the bar-tender empties the residual spillage collected in his drink mat into a glass. And which point the serious Bar Hopper raises a toast to everyone and downs it like a champ.

SHOOT THE BOOT A storied rugby tradition is when a player celebrates his first goal by drinking directly from his muddied cleats. Although cleats are not proper attire for bar hopping, you can mimic the thrill of victory by drinking from one of your own shoes.

CHUG LIKE A CHAMP

A great chug can be the stuff of legends. It can gather a crowd. It can inspire legions of fans. It can go to your head—in more ways than one. Here are some chugging techniques and some impressive chugging stunts to whip out as needed.

GENERAL CHUGGING PRINCIPLES

NO 1 WARMER IS BETTER Ice-cold beer, while great for sitting by the dock of the bay, can cause undue difficulty during a high-speed entry. So let it mellow to just below room temperature.

NO 2 FLATTER IS BETTER Carbonation is what makes beer refreshing and delicious. But the hero of taste is the enemy of chug. Allow your beer to flatten a little by letting it stay opened and untouched for a few minutes.

NO 3 PRACTICE MAKES AWESOME If you are intent on raising your chugging game, we recommend you practice with water. It's cheaper and less carbonated, and you can practice anytime. The idea is to become familiar with the chugging sensation, letting your body relax and controlling your reflex to swallow too much.

SHOW-STOPPING SHOTS

If you are looking to go out with a bang, then step up to any of these hardcore shots for some liquid bang in a glass.

THE BLACK SUNDAY SHOT

There's nothing sacred about this shot. Mix together
1 ounce of grain alcohol, 1 ounce of 101 proof bourbon,
and a splash of black cherry soda. The soda will distract you
from the burn just long enough for you to cry for help.

THE STUNT MAN SHOT

Popular with the rugby crowd, this is the masochistic spin
on a traditional tequila shot. You snort the salt, squeeze
the lime into your eye, shoot the tequila, and take your place
on the altar of awesome.

THE STATUE OF LIBERTY SHOT

Don't let the name fool you. This is much more idiotic
than patriotic. In short, this shot can cause serious physical—
not just emotional—damage. Take a double shot of a high-proof
spirit (such as 151, vodka, or Rumple Minze), then dip your
finger in it and light it on fire. Hold your flaming digit in the air
and drink the rest of the shot. There's an even more dangerous
grand finale: extinguishing the flame in your mouth.

"There are no limits.
There are only plateaus,
and you must not stay there,
you must go beyond them."

BRUCE LEE

EXPANDING

THINKING OUTSIDE THE BAR

We hope by now you can truly appreciate how bar hopping is more than an activity, it's a way of life. So it would stand to reason that a Hopper at heart would bring her skills to bear in a wide variety of other occasions as well. Of course, these skills need to be readapted and reapplied to these other opportunities. But for a seasoned Hopper, thinking outside the bar is no problem—especially with the help of this chapter.

The bar hopping mind-set really comes in handy in more places than just the bar. The following pages will break down some of the "nonbar" occasions for a Hopper to enjoy.

PROGRESSIVE DINNER PARTIES These are parties that move from house to house throughout the night. Each stop has another drink or dish to consume—often both. While huge in the 1950s, they had all but vanished by the 1990s. But today, a new generation of Bar Hoppers has taken the torch and is carrying it, along with food and booze, from house to house.

TAILGATES The pregame of all pregames before a big event is a veritable playground for the consummate Bar Hopper. It's a place where you can go from party to party without even leaving the parking lot.

HOW TO WORK A TAILGATE LIKE A PRO

By David Lamm, Tailgating expert

PAY ATTENTION TO DETAIL

Strike up a conversation with anyone. Take notice of someone wearing the jersey of a not-so-well-known retired player and comment how he was your favorite too. The ensuing conversation about said player can turn into an invite under the pop-up tent for drinks and food until the game starts.

PLAY A ROLE

Pretend to have traveled a long distance to come to this game. Fans will respect someone who has gone through so much to support their team too. This will also explain why you don't have your own tailgating gear with you. (The airlines frown upon claiming a grill as your one "personal item" to put in the overhead bin.) Just be sure you have adequate knowledge of the neighborhoods and surrounding areas of the place you claim to be from. Rather awkward if you can't come up with a valid answer when asked "Where did you go to high school?"

GO INTERNATIONAL

If you can sustain a believable accent through copious amounts of alcohol consumption without forgetting what accent you started with, pretend to be from a different country. This works especially well at football games, which are uniquely American and not played anywhere else. If you claim to be a fan of the game but say it in an eastern European accent, tailgaters will want to show you how tailgating is done correctly in America. Just don't go Kevin Costner in *Robin Hood* and fade in and out of the accent.

WRITE AN ARTICLE

Pretend to be a journalist writing an article about tailgating. Make up the name of the newspaper, magazine, or website if you need to. Most people will be eager to show you a good time in exchange for getting their name mentioned in an article. As a guy who owns a tailgating blog, I cannot tell you how many invites I have gotten to sample food and drink at a total stranger's tailgate party. Bring a pad of paper to complete the character and snap a few photos with your phone.

Learn more about tailgating like a pro
at David's website, TailgatingIdeas.com

BOAT PARTIES What do you get when you throw a few thousand sunburned revelers onto a body of cool water with drinks and party barges? Described by some as a "redneck yacht club," this party scene found on lakes across America is the perfect setting for Bar Hoppers to try out their amphibious skills—hopping from boat to boat, party to party.

FESTIVAL CONCERTS These sprawling outdoor palooza-zas are the stuff dreams are made of for music-loving Bar Hoppers. Multiple stages of live music, thousands of potential friends or mates, and one convenient location to stumble around. The only rub is the eye-gouging price of alcohol. A necessary evil for civilians, an opportunity for creative problem solving for Bar Hoppers.

CASINOS Casinos have grown from being dens of illicit behavior to massive, multi-billion-dollar, climate-controlled cities of illicit behavior. In other words, nirvana for a sea-soned Bar Hopper who knows how to work the system. The house may win, but the Hopper always rocks.

FREE GOODS IN SIN CITY

There was once a time when it was as easy to drink for free in Vegas as it was to bury a body. Unfortunately, these days the streets are full of families, the stages full of French Canadians, and the bars are full of fools paying full price. Here's how to Bar Hop in the mother of party towns—without losing your shirt.

HANG WITH THE LADIES

You either won the genetic lottery or you didn't. Vegas expert Rick Lax, author of *Fool Me Once: Hustlers, Hookers, Headliners, and How Not to Get Screwed in Vegas* explains it this way: "Clubs and bars in Las Vegas survive on guys paying full price—up to $50 covers just to get in." Dudes can try to surround themselves with females to avoid covers and lines, but make sure the ratio of XX to XY is at least 4 to 1.

BETTER YET, BE A LOCAL WOMAN

What tops being a girl? Being a hot townie girl, that's what. They bring the most word of mouth to the bar. According to Lax, "Local females are in high demand at the clubs—so much so, the clubs will pay for your cover, drinks, table service, and even comp you dinner and a personal escort to the club." It's good to be the queen.

SLOPPY WITH THE SLOTS

It's no secret the casinos make money when you part with yours. As long as you're gambling, they'll hook you up with freebies.

And, since the slots have hustled mankind for millennia, it's time to hustle them back. Lax suggests you put a dollar in a machine and wait for the waitress. Get your free drink, cash out your dollar, and give the finger to the one-armed bandit.

THE POKER PIMP

Slots not your style? Money not your friend? Cozy up to a $1/$2 poker table and order a drink for you and your posse. Then proceed to fold every hand. Repeat until you get asked to move your full belly out of the seat.

MASTER THE MIDGAME

Everyone has heard of the pregame, but pros break out what Lax calls the midgame. First, you go to a club early, when you can get in without a cover or a line. Shake moneymakers and drink waters. Then get your hand stamped and leave the club for the gaming floor. Load up on cheap drinks using steps 3 and 4 above. Then use your stamped hand to return to the club with your tank on full.

TALK TO THE TOWNIES

Sure, you're just in to do some liver damage and leave; but take the time to talk to the locals. You'll learn about hidden gems— casinos with good comps, dives with cheap drinks, and holes-in-the-wall with killer grub. Lax gives a good rule of thumb: "The crappier the place, the better the deal."

Get more inside tips from Rick Lax at his website, RickLax.com

SMUGGLING BOOZE

Bar Hoppers can't be limited by rules or cultural norms or laws. Thinking outside the bar means seeing what others don't, and doing what others can't. So when most people see a quiet movie night at the Cineplex, an afternoon at the bowling alley, or a even a day at the public beach, Bar Hoppers see the perfect setting for a perfect pregame.

DISGUISING In these tactics, the original container is kept intact but surrounded in various forms of camouflage.

SUPER SIZED
(to keep it hidden)

BEER
(to keep it awesome)

ICE
(to keep it cold)

BEER GULP Don't like soda or warm beer? This solves both. Place the can inside a supersized soda cup, top with ice, and insert the straw all the way into the can.

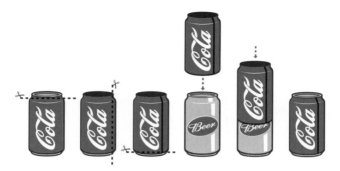

CAN SLEEVE This is a simple creation of a cover that fits over a beer can—magically transforming it into a benign can of soda. Nothing to see here, folks.

PAPER BAG An oldie but a goody. Simply place your container in a paper bag, twist around the top of the bag, and enjoy!

FLASKING Using a flask is often the gentleman drunk's favorite technique. What it lacks in large volume, it makes up for with the slightest bit of social acceptance. It's the difference between your grandmother hearing you got caught with a flask of rum at a concert and the cops impounding your prosthetic bladder of booze shaped like boobs (more on that below).

THE CLASSIC A metal flask, sometimes leather-bound, sometimes engraved
- **PRO:** The Classic is classy and perfect for bringing some fun to a highbrow affair.
- **CON:** It's an investment that can get confiscated quite easily.

THE SOFT PACK A flexible, refillable plastic bladder with a spout for easy access
- **PRO:** Can't be caught by metal detector; leakproof.
- **CON:** Takes some premeditation, too professional-grade to admit to owning.

THE HOMEMADE HOBO A Ziploc baggie filled with booze
- **PRO:** It's cheap and might evade a quick pat down.
- **CON:** May leak, may damage self-esteem.

SPIKED FOOD

Sometimes the best hiding place is in plain sight.
Or in this case—get ready folks—sight. Spiked foodstuffs offer
an entertaining way to bring a bit of booze to the event.

JELL-O SHOT CAKE

There's always room for boozed up Jell-O. The general rule
of sticky thumb is to dissolve 3 ounces of Jell-O in 1 cup of
boiling water, then add 8 ounces of cold vodka or grain alcohol.
Make enough at this ratio to fill a large cake mold. Chill, remove
from pan, and top with Cool Whip and sliced berries. The
heavenly outside belies the devilish interior.

VODKA GUMMY BEARS

These little treats will put some bear hair on your chest.
Soak as many gummy bears as you can find in a vodka
bath for three to five days. They will plump in size, soften in
texture, and kick you in the ass. Put them in a plastic bag
and sneak these sweet shots anywhere.

LIQUOR LOAF

Take a large loaf of crusty bread, cut a small hole and hollow
out the bread, then place a bottle of liquor inside, then put the
whole thing (hole side down) back into the paper bag from the
baker. Walk right past security with your bread-eating grin.

CRASHING

No bar in sight or party in the plans? What are Bar Hoppers to do? The answer is simple: make your own fun by crashing someone else's fun.

Truth be told: it's tough being the life of the party when your name's not on the guest list. That's why we've created a foolproof guide to crashing any event at any time. From weddings to keg parties, you'll never need an invitation ever again.

HOW TO PROPERLY CRASH A PARTY

Crashing is more than showing up. It's showing up *and* rocking out while fitting in without getting kicked out. Sound easy? Right, it's not. But here are some ways to get started.

ACT LIKE YOU BELONG Every good host lives in terror of forgetting the name and identity of an invited guest. It's up to you to seize upon this fear by boldly going up to the host the moment you enter the party and offering them a warm handshake. Adding a hearty, "It's so lovely to see you again," will ensure they'll play along out of fear they've forgotten who you are completely.

106

BRING SOME GIFTS No host can refuse a guest who comes bearing gifts. Just ask the Three Wise Men. They crashed the most exclusive celebration on the planet with just some gold, frankincense, and myrrh. The good news is, you don't even have to spend much money, so long as the host doesn't open your gift until long after you've drunk all of their imported beer. For a wedding, bring a nicely wrapped box. For a house party, put a soda bottle in a nice wine bottle gift bag (free at most wine stores) and put a bow on it.

DANCE WITH GRANDMA We mean this both literally and figuratively. Endear yourself to the room with an "oh, how sweet" gesture. Sure, it might draw a little attention your way, but it will make you so well loved they'll be blinded to the fact that you don't belong. Try an endearing gesture like dancing with an old relative, leading the conga line, or entertaining the kids' table with pratfalls.

MIND THE SMALL STUFF Humans are experts at ferreting out small differences and ignoring similarities. Don't give them any reason to think twice. For example, make sure you have the same color house cup at a college party by keeping a stash of every Solo color on the market in your car. If you are crashing a conference party, get the name tag. If you are crashing a Jewish wedding, get circumcised.

PEACE OUT

No matter if you're in a bar, casino, or crashed party, people are more prone to remember the last part of any experience— even more than the beginning or the climax. Here are five proven methods to try when making an unforgettable exit.

THE LOU GEHRIG

Get everyone's attention, take off your hat, and thank everyone for their support and their alcohol. Choke back some tears—and beers.

THE DEF COMEDY

Hold a beer bottle or full cup of your favorite beverage above your head. Dramatically drop it on the floor and exit stage left.

THE SWAYZE

Just be a ghost. One moment you're at the bar.
Then, *poof!*, peace out. Note: This is ruined if you attempt to spin pottery with anyone else in the room.

THE MAYOR

Shake hands, kiss babes, and make sure everyone gets one last good impression before you peace out.

THE COMPANY MOVE

This exit involves bringing a majority of the bar with you as you relocate to a B.B.B. (Bigger, Better Bar).

BAR HOPPING NOTES

Acknowledgments

The authors would like to thank: our talented lead contributors Michael P. Ferrari (www.michaelpferrari.com), and Ryan Murphy (www.askryanmurphy.com), as well as the extra help from Casey Andrews, Kristen Bowden, Kristen Cardilli, Jackie Grady, Christopher Hadnagy, Catherine Hsu, Sarah Lewitinn, David Lamm, Rick Lax, Elise McDonough, Mike Raleigh, and Mike Student. And, of course, we could not have hustled this book without Kate Willsky, Emily Haynes, and everyone at Chronicle Books as well as Stephanie Kip Rostan, Monika Verma, and the team at Levine Greenberg.

About the Authors

Ben Applebaum and Dan DiSorbo like to create seriously foolish books. Their other collaborations include *The Book of the Party Animal*, *The Book of Beer Awesomeness*, *The Book of Beer Pong*, and *The Fart Tootorial*.

Learn more about their shenanigans at
WWW.BADDIDEAS.COM.

ALSO AVAILABLE

FROM

BEN APPLEBAUM & DAN DISORBO